Macbeth

AND ALL THAT

Macbeth

AND ALL THAT

Allan Burnett

Illustrated by Scoular Anderson

BIRLINN

For Ossian and Ronan

First published in 2007 by
Birlinn Limited
West Newington House
10 Newington Road
Edinburgh
EH9 1QS

www.birlinn.co.uk

ISBN13: 978 1 84158 574 1
ISBN10: 1 84158 574 2

British Library Cataloguing-in-Publication Data
A catalogue record for this book is available from the British Library

Designed by James Hutcheson
Typeset by Iolaire Typesetting, Newtonmore
Printed and bound by Cox & Wyman Ltd, Reading

Contents

Prologue

It was nighttime in a creepy castle. As the wind howled through the courtyard, a figure emerged from the gloom of an archway. It was Macbeth, lord of the fortress.

He paused until he was sure there was nobody else about. Then he scampered silently across the flagstones and up the steps towards the guest bedchamber.

He stopped outside the bedchamber's heavy wooden door, his heart racing. Very carefully, he opened the door a bit, trying to make sure it didn't creak. Then, very gingerly, he put his head round it and peered inside.

There, snoring loudly, were Macbeth's guests – King Duncan and his men. Their armour and weapons were piled beside their beds.

Macbeth held his breath as he slid through the doorway and drew out a dagger from under his cloak. He inched his way across the room until he came to the bed where Duncan lay peacefully sleeping.

As he stood looking down at the defenceless king's face, Macbeth's heart pounded in his chest and his palms were slick with sweat. He hesitated for a moment.

Suddenly, Macbeth's dagger plunged deep into Duncan's belly, making a dreadful squelchy noise. Duncan groaned quietly for a second and then let out a long, empty sigh. The king was dead.

Macbeth looked down at the dagger in his hand. Duncan's blood was dripping from the blade and on to his clenched fist.

The other men were still asleep. Trying not to pass out or trip over anything, Macbeth crept out and then hurried down the stairs.

When he got back to his own room, Macbeth's head was spinning. He felt dazed and confused. He couldn't believe what had just happened. Had he really murdered the king in cold blood? Or was his crime just a nightmare?

Well, many people who have heard about Macbeth will tell you he definitely was not having a bad dream. They insist he really *did* kill Duncan as the king slept in his bed.

If you want proof, they say, just read the play about Macbeth's life written by William Shakespeare in 1605. The play is called, you guessed it, *Macbeth*.

According to Shakespeare, Macbeth slaughtered Duncan in his bed so Macbeth could steal his throne. But the consequences for Macbeth after committing such a cold-blooded murder were terrible. More terrifying than you can imagine. I mean really, really bad.

What many people don't realise is that there is more to the story of Macbeth than Shakespeare's play. Some bits of Shakespeare's play are correct, but other things didn't happen exactly as Shakespeare describes. After all, a play acted out on a stage is not the same thing as real life. Plus,

Shakespeare's play was written almost six hundred years after Macbeth was alive.

So, to find out the truth about Macbeth, you must read on. But be warned, this could be the most chilling history book you will ever read.

Our quest to uncover what really happened will take us back in time a thousand years, to the violent and bloody age when Macbeth lived. Along the way, you will be tormented by witches, haunted by ghosts and roared at by Vikings. But if you are tough enough to stick around, you will learn all sorts of amazing facts about what life was like in Macbeth's day.

You will also get to know Shakespeare's play inside out. It's not only a cracking good drama, but it contains vital clues that will help you work out whether the real Macbeth was a hero or a villain . . .

1

Son of life

Shakespeare's play tells us next to nothing about the facts of Macbeth's childhood. So to discover how Macbeth's story truly begins, we must first find out what modern historians have to say about him.

Historians have used fragments of writing from ages ago to try to piece together Macbeth's murky early years. These pieces of history come from centuries before Shakespeare was even around, let alone us.

They reveal that Macbeth's lifetime was an age of magic and sorcery, epic battles, romance and murder. This makes Macbeth sound extraordinary, but don't forget – Macbeth was a real person, just like you and me.

We are told that Macbeth was born a prince – okay, so he was *quite* like us. He grew up in the mini-kingdom, or province, of Moray in northern Scotland.

Macbeth's exact birthday is a mystery, but it was almost certainly some time during the year 1005.

The name Macbeth means 'son of life' in Gaelic. The original Gaelic spelling is Mac bethad.

Macbeth was a keen hunter and he had two greyhounds, which he took on expeditions into the forest with his dad. His dad also taught him how to be a warrior and use weapons like swords.

Macbeth learned languages too, including Gaelic, the native language of most Scots in those days, and Norse. Being able to speak different languages was vital to being successful in Macbeth's day.

Although Norse was spoken by many Scots, it was originally the language of the Vikings – and Norse is also another word for Viking. The Vikings were fierce warriors who had sailed to Scotland across the North Sea from Scandinavia and now ruled large parts of the country.

Macbeth also learned Latin, which was the language spoken by religious leaders. It was also used for important government business.

It was crucial that Macbeth learned lots of useful stuff like languages because his family were real big shots. In fact, his dad, Findlaech (pronounced 'Find-lay-ech'), was the mormaer of Moray. The word 'mormaer' is another way of saying that Findlaech was governor, or prince, of the province of Moray.

Moray was one of the most powerful and wealthy provinces in Scotland, although Scotland was known by a different name in those days. Can you guess what the nation was called when Macbeth was around?

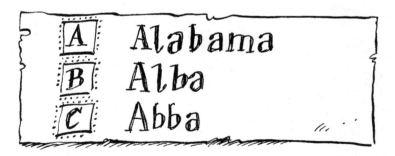

Well, it wasn't 'A', of course. Alabama is a place in the United States of America, and it didn't even exist when Macbeth was around.

7

It wasn't 'C', either. Abba are a pop group from the 1970s. Their music is ancient, but it is not as old as Macbeth. Besides, Abba come from Sweden in Scandinavia, so they are Vikings – not Scots.

That means the answer is 'B', Alba. In fact, Gaelic speakers still call Scotland Alba to this day.

Because Macbeth's dad's province of Moray was one of the most important provinces in the kingdom of Alba, a lot of people gave the Macbeth clan maximum respect. But there were others who didn't respect them at all.

In fact, there were a lot of greedy creeps around who just wanted to kill Macbeth's dad and seize control of Moray. Take the Vikings, for example . . .

2

The magic banner

The Vikings were always trying to steal and plunder things from the province of Moray – just like Wild West bandits.

Unlike Wild West bandits, the Vikings usually used boats instead of horses to do their looting. They sailed along the coast and whacked poor unsuspecting villagers and churchmen, and then they went back to their base. This was called raiding – and the Vikings loved it.

The trouble for Macbeth and his dad was that Moray was right on the Vikings' doorstep, so it got raided all the time.

Macbeth came face to face with the Vikings when his dad took him on tours around Moray – which was a big place. After all, being a mormaer was all about meeting and greeting your subjects and sticking up for them when the going got tough. Macbeth's dad had to try to help people along the Moray coast defend themselves against attack.

Learning how to stand up to Vikings was all part of Macbeth's education. If you ever get picked on by a school bully during your education, at least you know you will never have to deal with utter nutters like the Vikings. Unlike school bullies, who are all cowards deep down, Vikings were totally fearless – and armed to the teeth!

Anyway, when Macbeth was a young lad, Findlaech had a big battle with a Viking called Sigurd the Stout. As you can probably tell from his name, Sigurd the Stout was quite a chunky fellow.

Sigurd was also the Jarl of Orkney. Jarl is another way of saying Sigurd was an earl, or mini-king. Mind you, there was nothing 'mini' about Sigurd.

The Jarl of Orkney might have been chubby, but he was no slouch when it came to fighting battles. When he met Findlaech's army in Caith-ness he made sure he had his secret weapon with him – his magic banner. This was a flag that could de-stroy his enemies if he waved it at them. The flag had a picture of a raven on it. When it fluttered in the breeze, the menacing bird seemed to fly.

There was only one prob-lem with the magic banner: although it guaranteed vic-tory for Sigurd's army, the man who carried it was doomed to be killed during battle. This is exactly what happened when Find-laech and Sigurd's armies clashed.

The man carrying Sigurd's magic banner, known as the standard-bearer, was quickly struck dead during the fight. So Sigurd ordered another man to pick up the banner and continue waving it at the enemy. But the second standard-bearer soon got splattered.

Then a third man was commanded by Sigurd to pick up the magic banner. Guess what happened to him? Yes, he was killed too.

Now who wants the honour of carrying my banner?

Just when it looked like Sigurd might run out of standard-bearers, the magic banner delivered on its promise. Findlaech's army was defeated and Sigurd was victorious.

Amazingly, although he lost the battle, Findlaech survived to tell the tale. Not that he would have wanted to boast about getting thumped by a plump Viking.

So much for Macbeth's dad – what about his mum? According to medieval historians, who were known as chroniclers, she was called Doada (pronounced 'Doe-ada').

She might as well have been called Dodo, because almost all the facts of her life are extinct. We know next to nothing about her.

3

Creepy cousins

To underline how royal he was, Macbeth was allowed to go and stay with Malcolm II in his royal house. In fact, Macbeth might even have had Malcolm II as a foster father.

Fostering your children to other parents was very common in those days. It was a good way of building up trust and friendship between families.

The fact that young Macbeth had a foster home that he could be sent away to came in very handy in the year 1020, when a quarrel erupted over who should become the next Mormaer of Moray.

When Macbeth's dad dies, we need to know who will be in charge!

Trouble was, the crown of a mormaer did not pass directly to his son. The tradition was that the crown was passed around between different parts of the mormaer's extended family in a kind of democratic way.

In other words, the crown was supposed to be shared between different branches of the clan.

If that sounds confusing then don't worry. It confused a lot of people at the time too.

Take Macbeth's cousins, for example. They got into an argument with Macbeth's dad, who was of course their uncle, over exactly who should get the crown after him.

The argument became a brawl. The brawl became a riot. Swords were drawn, armour was bashed and heads and legs were probably chopped off.

Macbeth's dad was killed, leaving Macbeth needing the help and protection of his foster father more than ever. This would have shown Macbeth that the life of a ruler was dangerous and bloody. It was a hard lesson, and it must have affected young Macbeth's outlook on life.

Macbeth probably left Moray for a while, making for the safety of Malcolm II's royal court in the south. It must have been a lonely journey, because as far as we know Macbeth didn't have any brothers – at least none that survived childhood.

Malcolm II grew fond of Macbeth. In fact, Malcolm II trusted Macbeth so much that Macbeth was at his side when he had an important meeting with King Canute – the powerful ruler of the three kingdoms of England, Denmark and Norway – in 1031.

17

So Canute proved kings are not invincible – and that taught his silly subjects a lesson. Perhaps Canute told Malcolm II and Macbeth this story as they sat together around the fireplace during their meeting? Canute would definitely have taken a good look at Macbeth to see what sort of person he was dealing with. So what did Macbeth look like?

4

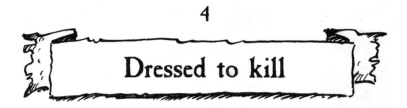

Dressed to kill

According to Shakespeare, Macbeth was dark and brooding. What does that mean? Well, imagine Macbeth with black hair and a grumpy face.

Remember, Shakespeare believed Macbeth was a really bad guy. By giving Macbeth a dark and grumpy appearance, Shakespeare was making him look the way people expected villains to look.

Heroes, on the other hand, were expected to have light or blond hair and a cheerful face.

Goodie

Baddie

Nowadays, we know that the colour of your hair, eyes or skin has absolutely nothing to do with whether you are a good or a bad person. Good people come in all shapes, sizes and colours.

In fact, Shakespeare's picture of Macbeth was probably wrong anyway. The truth is that we don't know for certain what Macbeth looked like.

Here are some other possibilities:

 Macbeth is des-cribed in a chronicle called *The Prophecy of Berchan* as tall and red-faced, with golden hair. This descrip-tion comes from a poem that was written for Macbeth, so  the writer probably wanted to flatter him by making him sound like a hunky hero.

 In some paintings, created long after Mac-beth lived, he was depicted in armour as a war-leader.

Macbeth has often been portrayed wearing tartan and a kilt. These paintings were also made long after Macbeth lived. Nobody can say for sure whether or not tartan and kilts were worn in Moray when Mac-beth was around.

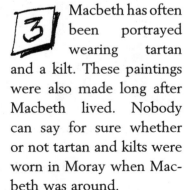

But one thing is certain, if kilts and tartans were worn, they were nothing like the Highland dress that people wear to weddings today. They were plain and simple.

Macbeth might have looked like a combination of all of the above. Whatever he wore, it must have been impressive and fearsome. Why? Because Malcolm II probably relied on Macbeth to go back north now and again to help keep the Vikings of Orkney at bay.

And Macbeth had another reason for being dressed to kill – when the job of Mormaer of Moray came up again.

Right, according to the rules, it should be me, Macbeth, who becomes mormaer.

Unfortunately, one of Macbeth's cousins disagreed. His name was Gillacomgain, and he jumped in to claim the job for himself, backed by some of Macbeth's other cousins.

As you can imagine, Macbeth was not pleased. His greedy, scheming cousins had seized the crown of Moray once before, by killing his dad. Now they were at it again.

While Macbeth quietly seethed with anger, Gillacomgain lived the high life as mormaer. But in 1032 Gillacomgain's fun suddenly stopped. He and fifty of his men were burned alive in a great fire. So how did it happen?

A. They were having a midnight snack of toasted marshmallows, but everybody leaned too close to the flame and their beards caught fire.

B. Somebody chased them all into a church, then bolted the door and torched the place.

Okay – the answer was obviously 'B'. The real question is, whodunnit?

Let's see . . . The killer would have to be someone who really hated Gillacomgain. Someone who wanted revenge for the murder of his dad, perhaps? Someone who believed the top job in Moray had been unfairly snatched away from him, possibly?

Hmmm . . .

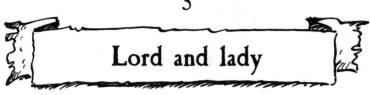

5

Lord and lady

As you have guessed, it was probably Macbeth who killed Gillacomgain. Macbeth got his hands on the leadership of Moray – he was mormaer at last!

But he also got his hands on something else – Gillacomgain's wife, Gruoch (pronounced 'Grew-och'). So, did he kill her as well? Or punish her? No – quite the opposite. He married her, probably in 1032, not long after he killed Gillacomgain, and Gruoch became Lady Macbeth.

This was a smart move on Macbeth's part because Gruoch's granddad had also been a king of Alba. Since Gruoch was related to royalty, the marriage made Macbeth all the more powerful.

What about romance? Did Gruoch and Macbeth actually *like* each other? Well, you would think Gruoch wouldn't have been too keen on a bloke who had just roasted her old husband. But, on the other hand, she might not have cared all that much for Gillacomgain anyway.

The thing is, marriages in those days were more about power than love. Macbeth realised that marrying Gruoch was a way of bringing the warring branches of his clan together, which made Moray more peaceful. Spreading peace and goodwill made Macbeth a popular leader.

There is no reason to doubt that Macbeth and Gruoch were reasonably happy together. Especially since Macbeth adopted Gruoch's son from her first marriage, Lulach.

Duncan lived at Dunkeld, which was close to the place where new kings of Alba were crowned – on the Stone of Destiny. He still had to be a fast runner to beat all the other people who wanted the crown for themselves to it.

The Stone of Destiny was kept at the town of Scone. (This has nothing to do with scones you eat with jam, of course. The place is pronounced 'Scoon'.)

Duncan got to Scone before any of his competitors. He was then crowned King Duncan of Alba. Good for him.

Trouble was, a lot of folk didn't think Duncan was the rightful heir to the throne.

Yes, you guessed it again, Mr and Mrs Macbeth wanted the crown! But to get their hands on it, they would now have to get past Duncan.

So what happened? To find out, you have to do some detective work. There are two sides to the story of what Macbeth and his wife did next, and you must decide which one is correct.

The first version of events is given to us by Shakespeare . . .

6

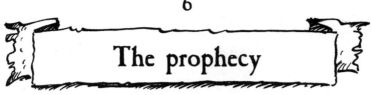

The prophecy

Thunder and lightning filled the air above the heath, or open moor. Unafraid of the storm, three witches were deep in discussion.

When shall we three meet again?

Upon the heath.

There to meet with Macbeth.

Then the witches flew away, through the filthy, foggy air.

Some time later, Macbeth was riding his horse across the heath. His friend Banquo was with him. They had just won a battle against an army of Vikings and were on their way home for a well-earned rest.

Suddenly, the three witches appeared before the two men.

Then the witches told Banquo that his descendants would one day become kings.

Macbeth and Banquo looked at each other, confused.

Then, as Macbeth and Banquo tried to figure out what was going on, the witches disappeared.

Macbeth had barely had time to get his head around this scary meeting when somebody else appeared. It was a messenger from King Duncan. He said that Macbeth had just been awarded a new title – Thane of Cawdor.

It looked like the witches had made a prophecy, foretelling future events. And the first bit had already come true!

Macbeth gulped. He was freaked out. But then he reflected on what had happened.

Then, as fate would have it, Duncan decided to pay a visit to Macbeth's castle in Inverness – which was in Moray.

Lady Macbeth believed this was a sign that the prophecy must come true. So she hatched a plan to murder Duncan, clearing the way for Macbeth to seize the throne.

When she told her husband about the plan, Macbeth wasn't happy about it. Killing the king was a dreadful crime. Then Lady Macbeth turned really nasty.

Eventually, Macbeth was persuaded to do the dirty deed. After all, deep down he *did* want to become king himself. But he felt very guilty about his decision. During the night, he sat alone and had a hallucination. He imagined he could see a blood-stained knife floating in front of him, pointing the way to Duncan's room.

'Is this a dagger which I see before me?' Macbeth said to himself. It seemed like the imaginary blade had been put there by some evil force that Macbeth couldn't control. It was commanding him to put aside his doubts and kill Duncan.

Macbeth was so horrified by the ghostly dagger that he desperately wanted to change his mind. But just as he was about to try to forget the whole thing, a bell suddenly rang. This was the signal from Lady Macbeth that Duncan's guards had been drugged and were now asleep. Casting aside his doubts, Macbeth crept into Duncan's room and skewered him with his dagger.

Then the really wicked part of the plan kicked in. Lady Macbeth framed Duncan's servants for his murder. While they were still sleeping, she planted bloody daggers on them – so it looked like they were the killers.

Next morning, two other noblemen turned up – Lennox and Macduff. They had come to Macbeth's castle to see the king, so Macbeth led them to Duncan's bed chamber. There, Macduff discovered Duncan's dead body.

Now the plan got very cunning. Before Duncan's servants could protest their innocence, Macbeth pretended he was in a rage about their 'crime'– and skewered them all.

But Macduff secretly suspected that all was not as it seemed. He believed Macbeth had something to hide – that was why Macbeth had suddenly slaughtered the servants before they could say a word.

After that, Duncan's two sons – Malcolm Canmore and Donald – became terrified that they would get whacked too. So they fled the country.

This was very convenient for Macbeth. With Duncan's heirs out of the way, the final bit of the plan came good. Macbeth took dead Duncan's place and was crowned King Macbeth of Alba. Then, he began to rule over the whole country.

So that's how Shakespeare explained Macbeth becoming king. But modern historians say that's not quite how things really happened. Time for version two . . .

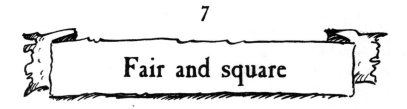

7

Fair and square

The historians' version of how Macbeth became king is very different from Shakespeare's. These historians have spent years carrying out detective work in archives and libraries, searching for facts about Macbeth. Shakespeare probably didn't know about most of this historical evidence when he wrote his play.

The historians' version of Macbeth's rise to the throne of Alba has no witches, no prophecies and no evil scheme to murder Duncan in his sleep. It also says nothing about Macbeth ruling the roost at Glamis or Cawdor – because there is no evidence he owned land or castles in these places.

But that doesn't mean this version is less strange or exciting than Shakespeare's. Far from it. To understand this side of the story, we need to turn the clock back to the moment when Duncan became high king of Alba. You also need to put yourself in Macbeth's shoes.

Now, before you start thinking this sounds suspiciously like Shakespeare's version of events you need to know one important fact. According to tradition, if an heir to the throne was blocked unfairly, like Macbeth believed he had been, then he was allowed to use force to try to win it over.

In other words, Macbeth was allowed to challenge Duncan to a battle to decide who should be king. And if Duncan was killed in the contest, too bad.

When it came to battles, Duncan was pretty rubbish – which is another good reason why Macbeth (and others) wanted rid of him. In fact, Duncan fought at least three big battles while he was king – and lost all of them.

BATTLE REPORT

ALBA V. ORKNEY – (1034 A.D. OR THEREABOUTS)

[AIM] DUNCAN WANTS TO GET TOUGH WITH NEIGHBOURING VIKINGS AND EXTEND HIS TERRITORY NORTHWARDS.

[ROUND ONE] BY SEA. DUNCAN TAKES FLEET OF SHIPS TO BASH THORFINN THE MIGHTY, VIKING RULER OF ORKNEY.

[OUTCOME] DUNCAN'S FLEET SUNK. DUNCAN ALMOST DROWNED.

ROUND TWO	BY LAND. DUNCAN TOOK HIS ARMY TO THUMP THE VIKINGS IN ROSS-SHIRE. VIKINGS GO BERSERK.
OUTCOME	DUNCAN'S SOLDIERS TURNED INTO MINCEMEAT. DUNCAN ONLY SURVIVED BY RUNNING FROM THE BATTLEFIELD.
FINAL SCORE	ORKNEY 2 — ALBA 0

BATTLE REPORT

ALBA v. NORTHUMBRIA   (1039 A.D.)

AIM DUNCAN WANTS TO EXTEND THE KINGDOM OF ALBA SOUTHWARDS

HERE IS A REPORT FROM OUR CORRESPONDENT AT THE SCENE...

DUNCAN, King of Scots, advanced with a countless multitude of troops and laid siege to Durham and made strenuous but ineffective efforts to capture it. A large proportion of cavalry was slain by the besieged and he was put to a disorderly flight in which he lost his foot-soldiers, whose heads were collected in the marketplace and hung up on posts.

ALBA

NEWCASTLE
DURHAM
NORTHUMBRIA
YORK

OUTCOME	MESSY. DUNCAN SCURRIED BACK HOME. THERE WERE QUESTIONS ABOUT WHETHER HE WAS FIT TO BE KING.
FINAL SCORE	NORTHUMBRIA 1 — ALBA 0

Macbeth saw his chance. According to reports, he started a rebellion against Duncan in the summer of 1040. To try to crush the rebellion, Duncan decided to meet Macbeth in battle on Macbeth's home turf of Moray.

That was a big mistake. Around 15 August, Duncan confronted Macbeth in battle near Elgin (at Pitgaveny, to be precise, which is on the Moray coast, about halfway between Inverness and Aberdeen). We don't know exactly how it happened, but Macbeth splattered Duncan's army good and proper. This time there was to be no escape for Duncan – he died from his battle wounds.

Macbeth wasn't king yet though.

But as soon as word got out that Duncan was dead, other people made claims to the throne. Rivals of Macbeth started coming out of the woodwork and racing towards Scone to try to beat him to it.

At the time, Macbeth was probably quite a popular choice. He had a very strong claim to the throne and he had proved himself a success in battle.

At least, that's what some historians believe. They prefer this version of events – which makes Macbeth sound more like a brave, honest guy – to Shakespeare's nasty version of how he got his hands on the crown.

But remember, there is still a lot that we don't know for sure. So think about both versions carefully before making up your mind about what sort of person Macbeth really was.

If you can't decide yet, don't worry – there will be more evidence for you to examine later on.

The next step in Macbeth's career was to try to be a good king. So did he succeed? Again, there are two sides to the story. First, let's go back to Shakespeare . . .

8

Throne of blood

Macbeth was now King of Alba. So far so good. But, according to Shakespeare, Macbeth believed he was surrounded by enemies. He thought he needed to splatter them before they splattered him. Simple . . . or so you would think.

The first enemy was Banquo, who had been with Macbeth when he had met the witches on the moor. Up until now, Banquo had been Macbeth's friend. But Macbeth kept thinking about the meeting with the witches. Remember, the witches had told Banquo that his descendants would become kings.

So Macbeth hatched another cunning plan. He invited Banquo to come to a feast at his castle – then secretly hired a couple of assassins to kill Banquo and his son, Fleance, while they were on their way.

The men were sent out on their mission, and they ambushed Banquo and Fleance as they rode across the moors. However, things didn't go according to plan. Banquo was bludgeoned, but Fleance fled.

When Macbeth found out that Banquo's son had got away, at first he was mad. And then he grew terrified – Fleance was sure to come back looking for revenge.

That night, the feast went ahead as planned. Macbeth's guests knew nothing of Banquo's murder yet – but they soon became suspicious that something was up.

Just as everyone was about to tuck into the meal, Macbeth had an unwelcome visitor. The ghost of Banquo turned up and sat in his seat!

The only person who could see the ghost was Macbeth. He was terrified and started talking to it. His guests became confused. Why was the king talking to an empty chair?

Lady Macbeth tried to smooth things over with the guests. She said Macbeth was feeling unwell and that it would be best if the guests went home. After the guests left, Macbeth decided the visit from Banquo's ghost must be an omen that something terrible was about to happen to him. So he decided to meet the witches again the next day to demand some answers.

Out on the heath the next day, the witches were waiting for Macbeth, while making a brew and chanting a magic spell:

Something wicked this way comes!

Right on cue, Macbeth appeared – and demanded some answers. So the witches conjured up three spirits to give him three clues about what would happen next:

Beware Macduff!

Nobody who was given birth to by a woman will harm you!

You will never lose your crown unless Birnam Wood comes to your castle at Dunsinane and attacks you!

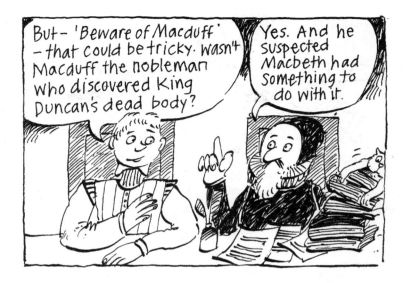

By now, Macduff had fled into exile to join Duncan's son Malcolm and get away from Macbeth. But Macbeth wasn't taking any chances. He wanted to make sure nobody from the Macduff clan could hurt him.

So Macbeth went to Macduff's castle and chopped up everybody in it – including Macduff's wife and children. What a nasty piece of work!

Things were now getting out of hand. Instead of feeling glad that Macduff's family were out of the way, Macbeth felt dreadful. He was on a killing spree and he couldn't stop. He felt more than ever that he was being controlled by some evil force.

Macbeth knew he was guilty of terrible crimes, and he drank lots of wine to try to make himself feel better. But it just made him feel more guilty.

Lady Macbeth didn't feel any better. Up until now, she had been egging her husband on – but all the killing was getting to her, too.

Lady Macbeth knew that ever since they had plotted to kill Duncan, she and Macbeth had blood on their hands. In fact, Lady Macbeth began sleepwalking and trying to wash imaginary bloodstains off her hands. The guilt was driving her mad.

So all in all, Macbeth's reign was a disaster. At least, that's what Shakespeare would have us believe.

But, as you've probably guessed, there's another way of looking at it . . .

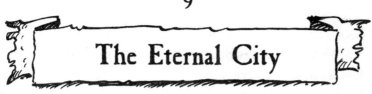

9

The Eternal City

According to historians, the facts of Macbeth's reign are different from Shakespeare's version of events. Again, there are no witches, spirits or ghosts.

Let's start with Dunsinane Hill, where Shakespeare says Macbeth had a castle. Dunsinane is only 12 kilometres from Scone, and Macbeth might have had a castle there after he became King of Alba, but historians don't know for sure.

In fact, it's very difficult to say much for sure about Macbeth's reign as King of Alba. Most of the evidence has been lost in the mists of time. After all, it *was* a thousand years ago!

Let's start with the bits of Shakespeare that other reports about Macbeth agree with. First of all, Macbeth definitely did have a few powerful enemies.

ENEMY NO. 4

Duncan's dad, Crinan. Abbot of the Abbey at Dunkeld.

He won't bother me again.

ENEMY NO. 6

General collection of people who invaded from Northumbria in the south to eliminate you.

They've all been splattered!

ENEMY NO 7.

Macduff. Sire, there is a rumour that he has it in for you.

Confiscate his castle and lands!

51

With so many enemies around, you might think Macbeth was a paranoid wreck as Shakespeare depicts him. But Macbeth seems to have been very confident and sure-footed when it came to dealing with his enemies.

In fact, it seems Macbeth was so successful that he could afford to leave his kingdom for a while and go on holiday. Some reports tell us that in the year 1050 Macbeth left Scotland and travelled to Rome.

These days, you can jump on an aeroplane and be in Rome in a few hours. But for Macbeth, travelling from Scotland to Rome took much, much longer.

It was a long, hazardous journey – around 2,000 kilometres. First you went by boat across the sea to either France or the Low Countries (known as Holland and Belgium today). Then you carried on on horseback through Switzerland, into Italy and along the road to Rome – or the Eternal City, as it was known.

The Eternal City had been the capital of the Roman Empire. This empire was long gone by the time Macbeth went there, but Rome's influence on the world was still huge because it was also the capital of the Church. Rome had been the most powerful city in the world for such a long time that people like Macbeth believed its importance would go on for ever – eternally. Even today, the place still goes by the nickname of the Eternal City.

Macbeth soon had other reasons for calling Rome the Eternal City – it seemed like it took an eternity to get there!

The trip lasted for many months and Macbeth needed men with him to fight off thieves along the way. He might have taken Lady Macbeth along, or she might have stayed in Alba to keep an eye on things.

But that doesn't mean Macbeth's enemies had disappeared. In fact, according to Shakespeare, they were busy plotting how to get rid of him . . .

10

Sound and fury

Shakespeare writes that Macbeth's enemies planned to kill him with an invasion of Alba. Leading the invasion were Duncan's son Malcolm Canmore and Macduff, along with a Northumbrian earl called Siward.

The invaders marched north and camped in Birnam Wood, near Macbeth's castle on Dunsinane Hill. Then the foot-soldiers were ordered to cut down tree branches and carry them, so they would be camouflaged as they crept up on Dunsinane Castle. It must have been very itchy and scratchy, even ticklish, but the soldiers had to try not to giggle in case they blew their cover.

Meanwhile, in the castle, nobody was feeling ticklish. The mood was bleak. Remember, as far as Shakespeare was concerned, Macbeth and his wife were now mass-murderers – and they were starting to think they deserved to be punished.

Lady Macbeth became so racked by guilt at her and her husband's murderous crimes that she committed suicide. Shakespeare doesn't tell us exactly what happened, but he does tell us that she gave off a loud shriek when she died. Perhaps she leapt to her doom from the battlements of the castle?

When Macbeth discovered what happened, he was filled with despair. He just wanted to curl up and die, and he said these famous words:

According to Shakespeare, Macbeth was so depressed by the sudden death of Lady Macbeth – and all the terrible crimes he had commited – that he thought his own life had become a waste of time. In this speech Macbeth says that no matter how much energy, or 'sound and fury', you put into your life, it doesn't matter. One day life will end – and become meaningless.

But there was still plenty of sound and fury to come, as the army of Malcolm, Macduff and Siward, covered in tree branches, rustled its way up the hill to the castle.

When Macbeth saw what was coming towards him he couldn't believe his eyes. The witches' spirits had said Macbeth would never lose his crown until Birnam wood came to attack Dunsinane Hill. But now the invaders' camouflage made it look like the wood really was attacking!

When the army reached the castle walls, a great battle followed. Cartloads of soldiers on both sides were skewered, splattered or torn limb from limb.

In the midst of all the bashing of helmets, clanking swords and blood-curdling screams, Macduff confronted Macbeth – and the two enemies had a duel.

Macduff told Macbeth that he had been born by Caesarean section – which is an operation to take a baby out of its mum without her having to push it out. So that means Macduff was not really given birth to by a woman.

The witches had tricked Macbeth! He barely had time to curse his bad luck before Macduff got the better of him in the duel. In a mighty stroke, Macduff swung his sword and lopped Macbeth's head off.

Now Macbeth was headless – just like the apparition that had warned him to beware of Macduff!

We must remember, though, that as Macbeth's head rolled away, it rolled across a stage and not the real ground – because Shakespeare's story is, after all, a play.

So how does Macbeth's dramatic death in Shakespeare compare with what historians tell us about the real-life plots to get rid of him? Time to find out . . .

11

The Seven Sleepers

The end of the real Macbeth's reign was very dramatic, but once again it was not quite the same as in Shakespeare's play.

In the year 1054, fourteen years after he had become king, Macbeth's enemies decided to try to get rid of him once and for all.

Let me see, who were these enemies? Perhaps Malcolm Canmore, son of murdered King Duncan?

Right! In his twenties, eager for the crown of Alba, itching to turn Macbeth into meatballs!

When the two armies clashed, probably at Dunsinane, there was a bloody battle. So Shakespeare was right to say that Macbeth did battle with Malcolm's army at Dunsinane.

In real life it was known as the Battle of the Seven Sleepers, because it took place on the day that the legend of the Seven Sleepers was celebrated. This legend said that in ancient times seven saints went to sleep in a cave and didn't wake up until centuries later.

Unlike the ancient saints, many soldiers in the Battle of the Seven Sleepers didn't wake up at all – because it's very difficult to wake up when you've got a sword through your belly! In fact, thousands of soldiers were splattered on both Macbeth's side and on Malcolm's side.

Right! Where's Macbeth?

Macbeth fled north to Moray, his heartland. He thought he would be safe from Malcolm there. He was wrong. Malcolm chased after him and the two men met in battle on 15 August 1057 at a place called Lumphanan. We don't know exactly what happened, but one way or another, Malcolm killed Macbeth in action.

Spookily, this was exactly the same date on which Macbeth had killed Malcolm's dad, Duncan, seventeen years earlier. Maybe Malcolm chose that day specially, to avenge his father's death?

After taking care of Macbeth, Malcolm rushed back to Scone.

But Malcolm was in for a nasty surprise. The spirit of Macbeth lived on . . .

12

Lulach the loser

Remember Lulach, Macbeth's stepson? Unluckily for Malcolm, no sooner was Macbeth out of the way than Lulach announced that he – not Malcolm – was the rightful heir to the throne.

Luckily for Malcolm, Lulach was not the sharpest of swords. In fact, his nickname was 'Lulach the Stupid'.

Lulach's reign was the shortest of any Scottish king – less than a year.

But that wasn't the end of the Macbeth clan. Lulach's son drew his sword and tried to stake his claim for the crown of Alba too, by fighting Malcolm.

Malcolm was too strong for him, though. The brave young fighter's family was captured, and his treasures and castle were confiscated. He was forced into exile.

Other Macbeth relatives tried to keep the fight going, but Malcolm only grew stronger. He became the all-conquering king of Alba and ruled for many years, from 1058 to 1093.

So is that how our story ends – with the defeat of Macbeth and his clan, and the victory of Malcolm? Of course not!

There's lots more to tell. For a start, we need to find out why the ghost of Macbeth still stalks the land of the living.

But before we find that out, there is one witches' prophecy that's still to come true . . .

13

Twists in the tale

In the final scene of Shakespeare's *Macbeth*, Malcolm is crowned king. But there is one piece of the puzzle yet to fall into place.

Remember Banquo? Before he was killed by Macbeth in the play, Banquo was told by the witches that his descendants would be kings. Or, as they put it, 'Thou shalt beget kings.'

So who were Banquo's descendants?

Some believe one of them is our very own King James VI of Scotland, who has just become James I of England.

72

It was very clever of Shakespeare to include topics like witches in his play, because he knew everybody – not just the king – was interested in them. In fact, as you have discovered, Shakespeare's play had lots of topics that were fascinating – and remain so today. Ambition, temptation, greed, dishonesty, murder, revenge, good versus evil, magic . . . the list could go on and on.

Sure, Shakespeare added quite a few twists to the tale of the real Macbeth. But these exciting twists and extra details also make *Macbeth* one of Shakespeare's very best plays.

And yet many people are afraid to even *watch* this play. Why? Because it is said by some folk that the play has kept the ghost of Macbeth alive – and he gets up to all sorts of evil deeds whenever it is performed . . .

14

Curses

Many people believe the play *Macbeth* is cursed. This might be because the spells chanted by the witches are said to be *real* black magic rituals. Or it might be that the real Macbeth thinks the play has unfairly painted him as a villain – and he's still mad about it!

It is said that the bad luck began on the eve of the very first performance of the play, which was entitled *The Tragedie of Macbeth*, on 7 August 1606. A young lad named Hal Berridge was cast in the role of Lady Macbeth. (Girls weren't allowed to perform on stage in those days.)

Before the opening night, young Hal was stricken by a sudden fever – and died. The show had to go on, of course. So it was left to Shakespeare himself to step into to the poor boy's shoes.

Your beard is putting me off, Shakespeare!

But there was worse to come. In 1672, there was a performance of *Macbeth* in the Dutch city of Amsterdam. The actor playing Macbeth used a *real* dagger for the scene in which he murders Duncan. And guess what? He killed the actor playing Duncan for real!

And the tragedies didn't just happen to people in the play. When a new production of the play opened in London in 1703, the city was hit by one of the most violent storms in its history.

A few years later, in 1721, a man watching a performance of the play decided to get up in the middle of a scene and walk across the stage to talk to a friend. The actors were so upset by his rudeness they drew their swords and chased him from the theatre. But they didn't realise he was a local bigwig, and he returned with some of his men to burn the place down!

That is nothing, however, when compared with the dreadful events of 10 May 1849. A performance of *Macbeth* in New York ended in carnage. The actor playing Macbeth was extremely unpopular with some members of the audience, who threw potatoes, old shoes and stink bombs at him.

A riot broke out – which was actually quite a common way for folk to express their disapproval of a play or an opera in those days. It was even regarded as a bit of fun.

But things got deadly serious when the police and the local army turned up and started shooting into the crowd. By the end of the night, around thirty people lay dead in the street!

America had more *Macbeth* madness in store. On 9 April 1865, President Abraham Lincoln enjoyed a pleasant afternoon on board a cruiser on the Potomac River. He read aloud to his friends the bits of the play that come right after the part where Duncan is murdered. Less than a week later, Lincoln himself was assassinated.

Over the years, the catastrophes and weird events have just kept piling up – a bit like Macbeth's victims! Check out what's been reported in the past hundred years alone:

1928: at the Royal Court Theatre in London, a large stage set fell down and seriously injured some members of the cast. And a fire broke out in the dress circle.

1930s: the role of Lady Macbeth was due to be played by a grand old dame of the theatre, but she died on the final day of dress rehearsal. Her portrait was hung on the wall until another production of the play opened – when it promptly fell down. Spooky.

1934: during a performance one of the actors turned mute on stage. Then his replacement developed a high fever and had to be put in hospital.

1936: Orson Welles, the famous American film director, produced a special stage version of the play called *Voodoo Macbeth*. The cast included a genuine witch doctor. After one theatre critic gave the show a bad review, he died

less than two weeks later. Did the witch doctor put a curse on him? Who knows.

1942: during one production, the actor playing Duncan and two actresses playing the witches all died. Plus the costume and set designer committed suicide.

1947: an actor was accidentally stabbed during the sword fight at the end of the play – and died from his wounds. His ghost is said to haunt the Coliseum Theatre in Oldham every Thursday, which is the place and day he was killed.

1948: the actress playing Lady Macbeth at a production in Stratford, Shakespeare's home town, decided to play the sleepwalking scene with her eyes closed. Guess what happened? On opening night, she walked right off the stage and fell almost 5 metres– the height of a lorry. Amazingly she got up, dusted herself down, and finished the show!

1953: famous American actor Charlton Heston starred in an outdoor production of *Macbeth* in Bermuda. On opening night, when Macbeth's castle was set on fire by the invading soldiers, wind blew the smoke and flames into the audience and they had to run away. But it was worse for poor old Heston. Allegedly, his tights had been accidentally soaked in kerosene – highly flammable oil – and he suffered severe burns to his leg and groin. OUCH!

And if you thought the bad luck must have run out after all these years of tragedy, you can think again . . .

1998: American actor Alec Baldwin starred as Macbeth in a production of the play in New York. During the fight scene at the end of the play, Baldwin accidentally sliced open the hand of the actor playing Macduff.

Some people say that the reason for all this bad luck is not actually the witches' spells. In fact, they say the real curse occurs when a person dares to utter the word 'Macbeth' in a theatre.

But there is a way to break the curse, which you should learn just in case . . .

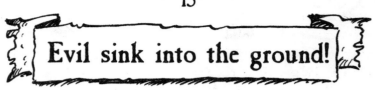

15

Evil sink into the ground!

Simply saying the name 'Macbeth' in a theatre is asking for trouble. It puts a curse on everyone involved.

At least that's what a lot of theatre folk believe. You can shout 'Macbeth!' all you want outside theatres, because the curse doesn't apply.

But that's not a whole lot of use when you're trying to do a version of the play – how on earth can you rehearse a play without ever mentioning its title or lead character?

Well, there is a way around it. According to tradition, if you are going to talk about Macbeth in a theatre then you should use one of the following nicknames:

If you make the ultimate mistake and do accidentally speak the word 'Macbeth' in a theatre, you must take action immediately to break the spell before it does some damage. Or else! Here are four options:

B

1 LEAVE THE THEATRE COMPLETELY...

2 ...PERFORM THE RITUALS AS IN... **A**

3 BEFORE KNOCKING TO ASK BACK IN, SAY THE WORST WORD YOU CAN THINK OF.

@'?//!

C TO WARD OFF MACBETH'S EVIL SPIRIT, QUOTE THIS LINE FROM SHAKESPEARE'S PLAY *HAMLET*:

Angels and Ministers of Grace defend us!

OR THIS ONE FROM SHAKESPEARE'S PLAY *THE MERCHANT OF VENICE*:

Fair thoughts and happy hours attend you!

D THIS ONE'S EASIER. TO BREAK THE CURSE SIMPLY SAY THE FOLLOWING PHRASE, LIKE A PRAYER.

> Thrice around the circle bound, evil sink into the ground!

Now, whether or not you believe *Macbeth* is truly cursed is really up to you. But the fact that lots of other people down the centuries have blamed it for all the bad luck you have just been reading about does seem to suggest that the ghost of the real Macbeth still might be with us – and he is definitely not a nice fellow!

So, could this mean that Shakespeare's villainous version of Macbeth is actually closer to the truth than some of the less wicked stories you have learned about him from historians? Well, perhaps it's time to find out . . .

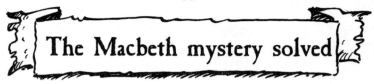

16

The Macbeth mystery solved

Macbeth is a very mysterious man. Of that there is no doubt. Our job in this investigation has been to try to discover what we can about the real Macbeth – to solve the mystery.

We have examined two versions of Macbeth's life. One is written by Shakespeare, and based on some medieval chronicles. Another is written by modern historians, who have looked at a wide range of evidence – not just plays or chronicles.

As you have discovered, the modern historians have given us some important, solid facts about Macbeth's life:

1 Macbeth born around 1005.

2 He became Mormaer of Moray.

3 He had a wife called Gruoch – Lady Macbeth.

4 He killed King Duncan at Elgin to become King of Alba in 1040.

5 He probably splattered Duncan's dad, Crinan, in 1045.

6 He beat off a Northumbrian invasion in 1046.

7 He gave land to the church at Loch Leven.

8 He went on a pilgrimage to Rome in 1050.

9 He fought another invasion from Northumbria in 1054.

10 He was defeated and killed at Lumphanan in 1057.

Using these key facts, we can say that Shakespeare got some important information wrong about where Macbeth was and what he was doing at particular times in his life.

For example, there is no proof that Macbeth murdered Duncan in cold blood while the king was asleep in Macbeth's castle. The evidence shows that Duncan was wide awake and got whacked in a fair fight during an open battle with Macbeth.

91

So our investigation has given us answers to the big questions about Macbeth – what the facts of his life are and what was he like as a person. Now it's time to put your knowledge into action . . .

Epilogue

Now that you know the truth about Macbeth, you can tour Scotland when you grow up and impress people with your knowledge – busting a few myths along the way. Just remember the facts you have learned in our investigation.

First up is Cawdor Castle, which stands between Inverness and Nairn. Many people believe this is where Macbeth murdered Duncan in his bed, because they think it must be the same as the 'Inverness' castle in Shakespeare's play. But you know that Macbeth actually killed Duncan in battle.

Then there is Glamis Castle (pronounced 'Glamz Castle'), near Forfar. Many people think the real Macbeth lived here because Glamis is mentioned in the play, but you know there is no evidence for that.

You can also take a ferry to the islands of Loch Leven, where there is an old stone tower. And you can impress other passengers on the way by telling them that the real Macbeth gave money for a church to be built on one of the islands.

Don't forget to include a visit to Birnam Wood and Dunsinane Hill in Perthshire. Many people believe this is the area where Macbeth was killed because that's how it happens in the play. You know that the real Macbeth probably did fight a battle there, but he was killed a few years later in a completely different place – Lumphanan.

The final query you might like to answer on your tour is, where was Macbeth's body laid to rest after he was killed? Where is the tomb to which his spirit goes for a rest when it isn't out haunting theatres?

Now that's an interesting question, and the answer remains a bit of a mystery. Some historians think Macbeth must have been buried in Perthshire. Others say Aberdeenshire. But there is a strong possibility that Macbeth's remains actually lie in the ancient burial place of Scottish kings – the island of Iona.

If Macbeth really is buried in Iona, then there might be another royal ghost who's not too happy about it. Because guess who else is buried there? Duncan, of course!

Maybe the two spirits are still arguing over what *exactly* happened on that fateful day in 1040, when Macbeth sent Duncan to his grave.

One thing's for sure, Macbeth's life and death is a lesson to all of us. Ambition can be a force for good, but it becomes a force for evil when our ambition is so strong that we will do *anything* to get what we want.

So does that make the real Macbeth a hero or a villain? You decide.